Spotlight on France

Bobbie Kalman

Crabtree Publishing Company

www.crabtreebooks.com

Created by Bobbie Kalman

For Peter Baker,
remembering the fun meals we had in France,
across the border from Karlsruhe

Author and Editor-in-Chief
Bobbie Kalman

Editor
Kathy Middleton

Proofreader
Crystal Sikkens

Photo research
Bobbie Kalman

Design
Bobbie Kalman
Katherine Berti
Samantha Crabtree (cover)

Print and production coordinator
Katherine Berti

Photographs
Circa Art: pages 24 (br), 25 (t)
Shutterstock: front cover, back cover, pages 1, 4, 5, 6, 7 (except mr), 8, 9, 10, 11, 12, 13, 14 (l), 16, 17 (tr, m, b), 18, 19 (t, b), 20, 21 (except tr), 23 (t), 26, 27 (t), 28, 29, 30, 31; Migel: page 7 (mr); amskad: page 17 (tl, tm); Luciano Mortula: page 18 (b); criben: page 21 (br); Anton Oparin: page 22 (t); Radu Razvan: page 22 (b); MagSpace: page 23 (bl); haak78: page 23 (br)
Thinkstock: pages 3, 14 (br), 15 (br), 21 (tr)
Wikimedia Commons: pages 15 (tr), 24 (tr), 25 (bl); Didier B.: page 19 (m); National Gallery of Art: page 25 (br); Wolfgang Staudt: page 27 (b)

t=top, b=bottom, m=middle, r=right, l=left, tl=top left, tc=top center, tr=top right, bl=bottom left, ml=middle left, br=bottom right

Library and Archives Canada Cataloguing in Publication

Kalman, Bobbie
    Spotlight on France / Bobbie Kalman.

(Spotlight on my country)
Includes index.
Issued also in electronic format.
ISBN 978-0-7787-0865-0 (bound).--ISBN 978-0-7787-0869-8 (pbk.)

    1. France--Juvenile literature. I. Title. II. Series: Spotlight on my country

DC17.K35 2013   j944   C2013-900671-0

Library of Congress Cataloging-in-Publication Data

Kalman, Bobbie.
 Spotlight on France / Bobbie Kalman.
    p. cm. -- (Spotlight on my country)
 Includes index.
 ISBN 978-0-7787-0865-0 (reinforced library binding) -- ISBN 978-0-7787-0869-8 (pbk.) -- ISBN 978-1-4271-9296-7 (electronic pdf) -- ISBN 978-1-4271-9220-2 (electronic html)
 1. France--Juvenile literature. I. Title.

DC17.K35 2013
944--dc23
                            2013003283

Crabtree Publishing Company

www.crabtreebooks.com   1-800-387-7650

Printed in the U.S.A./042013/SX20130306

Published in Canada
Crabtree Publishing
616 Welland Ave.
St. Catharines, Ontario
L2M 5V6

Published in the United States
Crabtree Publishing
PMB 59051
350 Fifth Avenue, 59th Floor
New York, New York 10118

Published in the United Kingdom
Crabtree Publishing
Maritime House
Basin Road North, Hove
BN41 1WR

Published in Australia
Crabtree Publishing
3 Charles Street
Coburg North
VIC, 3058

Contents

This old painting shows the Louvre Museum in Paris as it looked in the early 1800s (see page 18).

Welcome to France!

France is part of the **continent** of Europe. A continent is a huge area of land. Earth's other continents are Asia, Africa, North America, South America, Antarctica, and Australia/Oceania.

The seven continents are shown on the map below. Find the names of Earth's five oceans on this map.

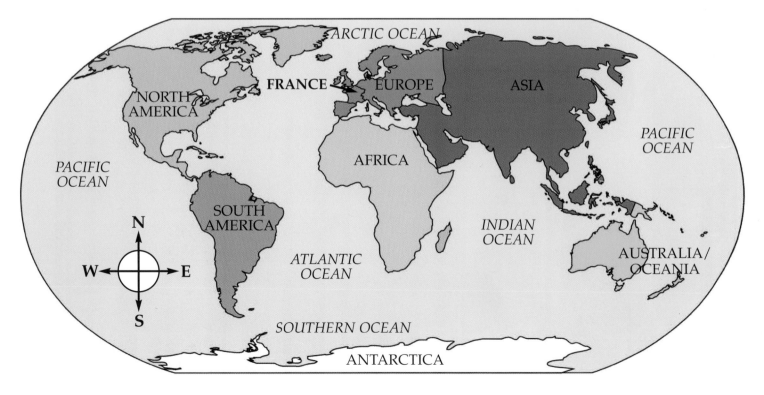

Where is France?

France is one of the largest **countries** in Europe. A country is an area of land with borders. France shares land borders with Belgium, Luxembourg, Germany, Switzerland, Italy, and Spain. The English Channel borders France in the north. The Atlantic Ocean is to its west, and the Mediterranean Sea is to its south. Other places around the world also belong to France (see pages 16–17).

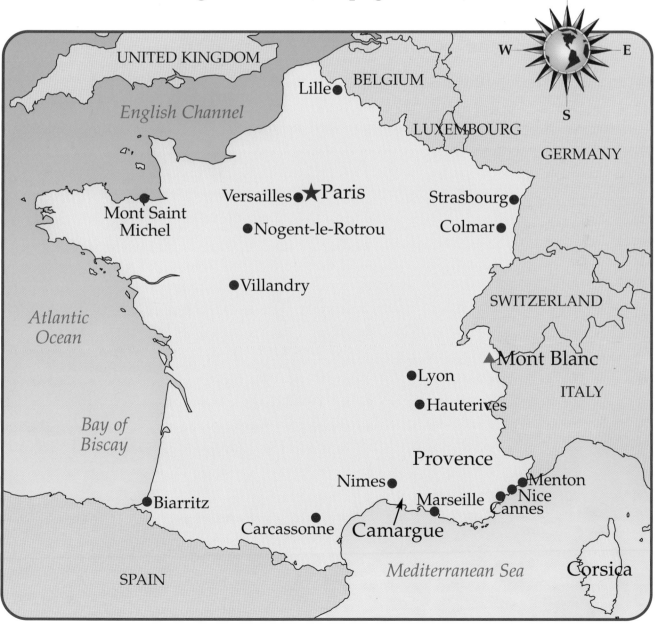

UNITED KINGDOM

N
W   E
S

BELGIUM

Lille●

English Channel

LUXEMBOURG

GERMANY

Versailles● ★Paris

Strasbourg●

●Nogent-le-Rotrou

Colmar●

Mont Saint Michel

Atlantic Ocean

●Villandry

SWITZERLAND

▲Mont Blanc

●Lyon

ITALY

●Hauterives

Bay of Biscay

Provence

Nimes●

●Menton
Nice
Cannes

Marseille●

●Biarritz

Camargue

Carcassonne●

Mediterranean Sea

Corsica

SPAIN

France at a glance

France is a land of many wonders. As well as being one of the largest countries in Europe, it is also one of the oldest. France is famous for its fine art, new fashions, beautiful landscapes, delicious foods, and exciting cities, especially Paris, which is the capital city.

The Eiffel Tower in Paris is France's best-known landmark. It was designed by Gustave Eiffel, a French engineer. When it was finished in 1889, it was the world's tallest structure. Each year, millions of tourists climb its 1,652 steps or ride up its 100-year-old elevator to get a good view of Paris.

Parlez vous
Francais?

☐ oui ☐ non

French is the official language of France, but people who have moved there from other countries speak other languages, as well. The sign above asks if you speak French. Is your answer oui (yes) or non (no)?

France's flag has three colors—blue, white, and red. This boy's face is painted in these colors, but he is not part of the French flag!

Most of the people in France follow the Roman Catholic religion. There are Catholic churches in every French town and city. The most famous is Notre Dame Cathedral in Paris.

Once ruled by kings, France is now a **republic**. A republic is governed by an elected government instead of a king or queen. France celebrates its history on National Day, also known as Bastille Day, with fireworks and a big parade.

France is part of the European Union, or EU, an organization of countries that support one another. The euro is the **currency**, or money, used in the countries that belong to the EU.

Beautiful landscapes

France is a beautiful country with a variety of landscapes. It has majestic mountains, deep **valleys** carved by rivers, rocky **cliffs**, and sandy beaches. Lush forests cover more than one quarter of the country. France also has many islands. Some, such as Corsica, are close to France, and some are on other continents. France is like a natural work of art for people, like this family, to enjoy!

The island of Corsica is in the Mediterranean Sea, south of France. It has high mountains and beautiful beaches. This picture shows the town of Évisa.

Lavender flowers cover some fields in Provence, a region in the south. In the distance are forests and hills.

Mont Blanc, in the French Alps, is the highest mountain peak in Europe.

French waters

The Atlantic Ocean touches France along its western **coast**, and the Mediterranean Sea is to its south. A coast is an area where water meets land. One of the most popular coasts is the French Riviera, which is along the Mediterranean Sea. Two of the cities along this coastline are Marseille, France's oldest city, and Nice. Within France are many rivers and lakes. The five biggest rivers are the Loire, Seine, Rhône, Garonne, and Rhine.

Nice has beautiful beaches and mild temperatures all year.

Biarritz is a city located on the Atlantic coast in southwestern France. Tourists flock there to enjoy the beautiful beaches. Biarritz has also become popular with surfers from around the world.

The Seine River is an important waterway that flows through Paris and ends at the English Channel. A small copy of the Statue of Liberty stands in the Seine River in Paris.

The Statue of Liberty in New York City was a gift from France.

Colmar has canals that run through the city. People call it "Little Venice" because it reminds them of Venice, Italy, a city with many canals.

Animals in France

Many wild animals live in France. Some live on a wildlife preserve called the Camargue. The Camargue is a large **river delta**, an area that contains shallow lakes and flat **marshes**. Marshes are low areas that are flooded for parts of the year. The Camargue is home to more than 400 **species**, or types, of birds. Its ponds provide a **habitat**, or natural home, for the greater flamingo and the Camargue horse.

These flamingos live in the waters of Camargue.

Camargue horses are some of the oldest breeds of horses in the world. For centuries, these horses have lived in the wild Camargue marshes. Camargue horses have black skin under their white hair. They are born with dark brown hair that turns white.

Wild boars live all across Europe, including France. They can be extremely fierce! These animals use their powerful tusks as weapons. People often hunt them and sell their meat to butcher shops and restaurants.

tusk

These coypus live in burrows beside rivers in the south of France. They feed on river plants.

(above) Alpine marmots live high up in the meadows of the French Alps. They are excellent diggers that can carve burrows into the sides of mountains.

(left) Chamois mountain goats live in the rocky areas of the French Alps. They are part goat and part antelope.

Long ago to today

For thousands of years, people have lived on the land that is now France. They came from different parts of Europe, including Italy, Scandinavia, and England. For more than 100 years, many battles were fought between France and England over the throne of France. In 1429, a young woman named Joan of Arc led the French army to victory, allowing the French king to claim the throne. Afterward, French explorers traveled the world and claimed faraway lands as **colonies** for France. A colony is a territory under the control of another country.

This statue of Joan of Arc stands in Paris near the spot where she was wounded fighting the English in 1429.

King Louis XIV, dressed in blue, was known as Louis the Great, and the Sun King. He ruled from 1643 to 1715. He was the most powerful king in France's history.

The French Revolution

Near the end of the 1700s, life was very difficult in France. Times were hard for most people, and they resented the wealthy **nobles**. On July 14, 1789, the French **Revolution** started when people captured the Bastille prison in Paris in order to get weapons. For ten years, there was a violent struggle to make France a republic. Then, Napoleon Bonaparte became France's **emperor**. An emperor is a powerful ruler.

Napoleon Bonaparte was emperor of France from 1805 to 1815. He fought wars with countries such as Italy, Egypt, England, and Russia.

Napoleon Bonaparte

Napoleon built a strong government and improved people's lives, but he also started many wars. In 1815, he was defeated by England and sent to live in **exile** on St. Helena Island, where he died six years later. After Napoleon, France was once again ruled by kings, until it became a republic in 1871. Today, the country is run by a president, who shares his or her power with a prime minister.

*In the 1900s, France was involved in two world wars. During World War II, Germany **occupied**, or took control of, France. Millions of people died, and the war left France with many challenges.*

Faraway French lands

Chateau Frontenac in Quebec City

Quebec is Canada's largest province. It was under French rule until 1763. Its official language is French. The islands of Saint Pierre and Miquelon, off the coast of eastern Canada, still belong to France.

French Polynesia is made up of groups of islands in the Pacific Ocean. Tahiti and Bora Bora are some of the best-known islands. Maupiti Island, above, is near Bora Bora.

Today, France's territory stretches around the world, but France once controlled many more colonies. Until the mid-1700s, parts of Canada and the United States belonged to France. France also ruled colonies in Africa, the Middle East, and East Asia.

Footprints around the world

French Guiana, in South America, is the largest of France's overseas territories. Most of France's other overseas territories are islands. Guadeloupe and Martinique are two French islands in the Caribbean, and Saint Pierre and Miquelon are islands off the Canadian province of Newfoundland. Mayotte and Réunion islands are in the Indian Ocean. Tahiti and 129 other islands make up the territory of French Polynesia in the Pacific Ocean.

Mardi Gras, or Carnival, is celebrated in France (see page 23), as well as in the French territories around the world. The two children on the left are celebrating Mardi Gras in French Guiana. They are part of the Carnival parade that takes place every year. The girl on the right is celebrating Mardi Gras in New Orleans, Louisiana. Mardi Gras reminds people in New Orleans of their French roots.

Martinique, shown above, is a Caribbean island that belongs to France. Guadeloupe is another.

Exciting cities

The Avenue des Champs-Élysées in Paris is the most famous street in France. It ends at the Arc de Triomphe, which was built to honor the victories of Napoleon Bonaparte.

Arc de Triomphe

France's major cities are filled with amazing structures and interesting buildings. Museums, art galleries, wonderful cafés and restaurants, and beautiful gardens also make French cities exciting places to visit. Paris, France's capital, is famous for the Eiffel Tower (see pages 6 and 11), the famous street called the Champs-Élysées, and the Louvre, an enormous art gallery.

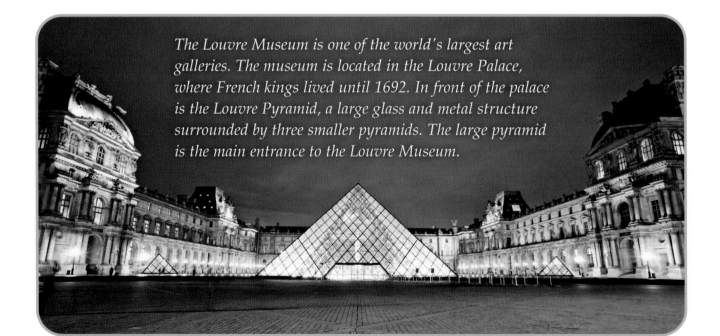

The Louvre Museum is one of the world's largest art galleries. The museum is located in the Louvre Palace, where French kings lived until 1692. In front of the palace is the Louvre Pyramid, a large glass and metal structure surrounded by three smaller pyramids. The large pyramid is the main entrance to the Louvre Museum.

Lille is situated on the Deûle River, near France's border with Belgium. This picture shows the Grand Place located in the heart of the city, the busiest part of Lille. It has historic buildings, shops, and restaurants.

Strasbourg looks like a beautiful work of art. The city is located on the Ill River, which flows into the Rhine River on the border with Germany. Most people who live there speak German as well as French.

Lyon is known as one of the best places in France for fine food. The farmland around Lyon produces a great variety of fresh fruits and vegetables, from which chefs create delicious dishes.

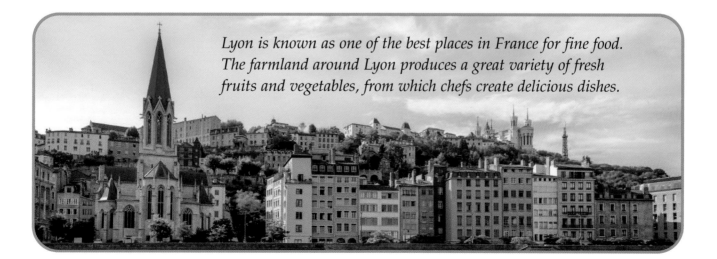

The people of France

French people are known for their *joie de vivre*, or love of life. They enjoy eating fine foods, wearing fashionable clothes, playing many kinds of sports, and celebrating special days with family and friends. Families also enjoy traveling around the world, as well as going sightseeing in their beautiful country. They enjoy hiking, swimming, and skiing.

(above) These girls attend a university in Paris. Before they were accepted to university, they had to pass a very difficult exam called the baccalauréat. They studied for two years to pass this exam.

(left) Many children who live near the French Alps learn to ski when they are young.

This man is a sheep farmer. He takes his lambs and sheep to the meadow to feed on grass.

Immigrants from many countries have moved to France. Fatoumata Diawara, born in Ivory Coast in West Africa, is a musician who now lives in France.

Celebrating culture

Paris is famous for its fashions. This model is wearing clothes by Chanel, a fashion house started by French designer Coco Chanel.

Culture is the way we live. It is the clothes we wear, the foods we eat, the music we enjoy, the stories we tell, and the ways we celebrate. The people of France take part in many kinds of sports and music and are famous for their art. The most exciting part of France's culture, however, is how people celebrate it today.

Many holidays

The French calendar is filled with *fêtes*, or festivals, which are celebrated with tasty food, colorful decorations, loud music, and exciting games. Some *fêtes*, like Christmas, are traditional religious holidays. Others, like Bastille Day and the medieval festival in Nogent-le-Rotrou, celebrate history.

People who live in Nogent-le-Rotrou celebrate a medieval festival at Saint-Jean Castle. They dress in historic costumes, play old musical instruments, hold parades, and demonstrate crafts from that time.

In February, the city of Nice holds the twelve-day Mardi Gras Carnival, one of the largest festivals in the country. "Mardi Gras" means "Fat Tuesday," the last day that people can eat rich foods before Lent, the six-week period before Easter. People dress in fabulous costumes and hold parades and parties.

The Lemon Festival takes place in Menton, in the south of France, between mid-February and early March. The festival attracts over 250,000 visitors. Hundreds of thousands of lemons and oranges are used to create castles (left) and statues, such as the **sphinx** above.

Famous artists

Some of the world's greatest artists lived in France. Many were French, but some moved to France from other countries. Until the 1700s, French artists painted like artists in other countries. After that time, they began to introduce other art styles to the world.

The Impressionists

Artists known as the Impressionists did not paint realistic pictures. They created their own **impressions**, or ideas, of how things looked. Famous Impressionists include Claude Monet, Pierre Auguste Renoir, Paul Gauguin, Edgar Degas, and Mary Cassatt. These pages show some of the works of these artists who lived in France.

Girls at the Piano *was painted by Auguste Renoir in 1892.*

(right) Mary Cassatt was an American painter who moved to France and lived there for most of her life. The painting on the right is called The Child's Bath. *Cassatt painted it in 1893.*

Paul Gauguin used strong colors and shapes in his paintings. He lived in Tahiti for many years, where he painted this picture.

Edgar Degas is best known for his pictures of ballerinas. This painting, called Girl Taking a Bow, *was painted in 1878.*

Woman with a Parasol *was painted by Claude Monet in 1875. The picture is of his wife and son.*

Amazing buildings

Like the paintings of French artists, the buildings in France are also works of art. Many were built long ago. Some of France's most magnificent buildings are its huge churches called cathedrals, which are decorated with stained glass, wall paintings, and stone carvings showing religious scenes. **Castles** and **palaces** are other old buildings that people love to visit. Take a tour of these famous buildings on pages 28–29!

Notre Dame is a Catholic cathedral in Paris. It is the most famous of all cathedrals. This beautiful church is located on the Île de la Cité, a small island in the heart of Paris. The cathedral is on the Left Bank of the Seine River.

Mont Saint-Michel was built more than 1,000 years ago by Christian **monks**, or religious men who devoted their lives to prayer. The **monastery** sits on top of a rocky island. The island is completely surrounded by water when the **tides** are high. At other times, soft sand surrounds the island. A road was built across the sand and water to allow people to reach Mont Saint-Michel.

The Arena of Nîmes was built by the Romans around 70 CE for events such as **chariot** races. Chariots were two-wheeled horse-drawn vehicles. Since 1863, the arena has been a stadium for bullfights. It can seat over 16,000 spectators. The statue in front is of a **matador**, or bullfighter.

Castles and palaces

The castle of Villandry is one of the most visited castles in France. People say it has the most beautiful gardens in the world!

Many of France's castles and palaces were built hundreds of years ago. The castles were large homes that were constructed with thick walls to keep people safe from enemy attack. Palaces were the homes of kings or other important persons. They had richly decorated rooms with luxurious furniture. Today, France's greatest palaces are museums.

The Palace of Versailles was built in the 1600s near Paris. During the time of Kings Louis XIII, XIV, and XV, it was the center of power in France. The many buildings contain hundreds of rooms and apartments where thousands of people, including the king and queen, politicians, and many servants lived. The palace is surrounded by beautiful gardens with fountains.

Carcassonne is a castle with a town built around it. The city has two outer walls with towers to prevent attacks. The castle has its own **drawbridge**. A drawbridge is a bridge that can be pulled up to prevent people from entering the castle or to allow boats to sail in the **moat**, or water that surrounded the castle.

The Palais Idéal is in the village of Hauterives in southeast France. This fantasy palace was built in the 1800s by Ferdinand Cheval, a postman. It is made out of the stones that Cheval collected while delivering mail. Many people visit the palace each year to admire this fascinating work of art.

French food

Many of the foods we love to eat came from France, such as french fries, french toast, crepes, croissants, quiches, and french bread called baguette. People in each part of France enjoy their own special foods. People who live near oceans, for example, may eat more seafood. Today, many foods from other countries are also found in French restaurants.

French fries have become a favorite food all over the world.

This mother and daughter are preparing crepes, which are thin pancakes. They are often folded or rolled and served with different fruit fillings.

French toast is bread dipped in egg and fried.

A quiche is a pie made with eggs, cheese, and ham, or different kinds of vegetables.

brie

Roquefort

French cheeses are delicious. Brie and a blue cheese called Roquefort are cheeses you might know.

This submarine sandwich is made using a baguette.

This family is enjoying a healthy lunch of fruits, salads, quiche, and long sandwiches on baguettes.

Glossary

Note: Some boldfaced words are defined where they appear in the book.

chariot A vehicle on two wheels pulled by horses

cliff A tall, steep wall of rock at the edge of an ocean or sea

coast Land that is beside an ocean

colony A place that is controlled by a faraway country

culture The customs, beliefs, and way of life of a group of people

currency Money used in a country

drawbridge A bridge that can be raised and lowered

emperor A ruler with great power over many countries and people

exile The state of being barred from one's native country

habitat The natural place where a plant or animal lives

monastery A place where religious men or women live, work, and pray

noble A person with a high social ranking or title

revolution An overthrow of a government through force

sphinx A large statue in Egypt with a human's head and lion's body

tide The alternate rising and falling of an ocean or sea, usually twice a day at a particular place

valley A low area of land between mountains or hills

moat A deep ditch around a castle, which is often filled with water to help keep out attackers

Index